EVERY PICTURE
TELLS A STORY

EVERY PICTURE
TELLS A STORY

ADVENTURES IN AUSTRALIAN ART

From the collection of the National Gallery of Australia, Canberra

John Ross with Anna Booth

CRAFTSMAN HOUSE

John Ross is an author and publisher. He was Editor-in-Chief of *Chronicle of the 20th Century* and *Chronicle of Australia* and has written many books, including *One People, One Destiny: The Story of Federation.*

Anna Booth is a researcher who lives in Canberra. Regular visits to the National Gallery of Australia delight and inspire her.

First published in Australia in 2008
by Craftsman House
an imprint of Thames & Hudson Australia Pty Ltd
Portside Business Park,
Fishermans Bend, Victoria, 3207
ABN: 72 004 751 964

www.thameshudson.com.au

ISBN: 9780980354034

National Library of Australia Cataloguing-in-Publication entry

Ross, John, 1938-
Every picture tells a story : adventures in Australian art / John Ross

1st ed.
ISBN: 9780980354034 (pbk.)

Includes index.
Bibliography.

For primary/secondary school age.
Australia–History–Pictorial works.

994.00222

All images in *Every Picture Tells A Story* are from the collection of the National Gallery of Australia. Thames & Hudson gratefully acknowledges the support and assistance of the Gallery and its staff.

Design: Adrian Saunders.
Production: Imago Australia Pty Ltd
Printed in Singapore

Contents

Artist listing

Introduction

EVEN BEFORE GOVERNOR Arthur Phillip stepped ashore at Sydney Cove in 1788 to found the first Australian colony, European artists had been at work. They had been out with Captain James Cook in 1770 and had made pictures of the trees, the animals, the landscape and the people of the great southern continent of Australia. They were like today's news photographers, making visual records, and they continued to show the progress of and the happenings at the tiny settlement at Sydney Cove.

So it has been throughout Australia's history down to today—the big events and the big themes of our national story have always been the subject of artistic interpretation.

Paintings were made of the threats that the land itself presents—flood, bushfire, drought, distance and loneliness. The dramatic painting by William Strutt of *Black Thursday* brings out the full terror and destructive power of a bushfire in the tall forests of Victoria.

Noel Nicolson's *Flash flood* shows a rush of water after a river has burst its banks. People died in such floods—87 of them on one night on the flats of Gundagai.

Wool drays by S. T. Gill portrays a team of bullocks struggling on rough terrain to get a load of wool bales to its destination. The photograph by J.W. Lindt of a bullock team carting wood shows the strength of the team and the flamboyant pride of the bullocky, with his mighty whip.

Sam Byrne's picture *Rabbit plague - round-up into old mine* is a memory of the scourge of rabbits across the land, and also evokes the harsh realities of life in the Australian outback.

Sam Byrne, *Rabbit plague round-up into old mine*, c. 1962

Artists have also captured the great characters and events of history. Nicholas Chevalier presented a tragic story of exploration in *Return of Burke and Wills to Coopers Creek.*

No one has represented the bravado, in life and death, of the bushranger Ned Kelly better than Sidney Nolan in his *Ned Kelly* series, painted in the late 1940s.

The massive painting *Opening of the first Federal Parliament,* by Tom Roberts, remains an enduring image of Australia's Federation in 1901.

The overwhelming sadness of war is seen in Nolan's picture *Head of a soldier,* while there is heroism and nobility in *Blinded soldier,* a photograph taken during the battle to stop the Japanese advance in New Guinea in World War 2.

Australia's social and industrial development is illuminated in art by famous paintings such as Tom Roberts *Allego con brio, Bourke Street west,* which captures the development of the city of Melbourne.

The stresses of living in modern Melbourne (or any big city) are seen in Jan Senberg's *Port Liardet,* and a famous landmark is reflected in Eric Thake's amusing *An Opera house in every home.* Howard Arkley captures the comforting peculiarity of Australian suburbia in his *House and garden, western suburbs, Melbourne.*

Howard Arkley, *House and garden, western suburbs, Melbourne*, 1988 (detail)

Ethel Spowers evokes our obsession with sport in *Football,* and our love of the beach is shown in *Australian surf club, 1936* by Gert Sellheim.

The great wealth of Australia came first from gold and wool, later supported by oil, minerals and manufacturing. Life on the goldfields is seen in S.T. Gill's *Cradling Forest Creek,* while George Lambert's *Weighing the fleece* captures both the romance and the importance of the wool industry. Our pioneering efforts continued all the way to inhospitable Antarctica, chillingly depicted in Jan Senbergs' *Antarctic night.*

There have been pictures for as long as there have been people in Australia. Aboriginal and Torres Strait Islander people have lived here for tens of thousands of years, and during all that time they have made images of the ancestral spirits of their dreamtime—like Wandjuk Marika's *The Birth of the Djang'kawu children at Yalangbara.* The indigenous art of Australia is part of the oldest continuing living culture in the world.

That was the beginning of the pictorial and historical journey that is told in *Every Picture Tells a Story: Adventures in Australian Art.*

Gert Sellheim, *Australia surf club*, c.1936

1. How the first Australians got here

Wandjuk Marika (1927–1987)
The birth of the Djang'kawu children at Yalangbara, 1982
Rirratjingu people, North East Arnhem Land
Ochre on eucalyptus bark.
147.5 x 66.0 cm
National Gallery of Australia

THERE ARE BEAUTIFUL paintings in caves and on rock walls all over Australia. The ancestors of today's Aboriginal people made them long, long ago.

More than sixty thousand years ago, when the seas were lower than they are today, groups of people crossed over a bridge of land from Asia to northern Australia. When the seas rose Australia was cut off, and developed its own unique local plants and animals. The rising water also covered a southern land bridge, and Tasmania became an isolated island.

These first inhabitants of Australia moved from place to place to find food and water and sometimes gathered in their favourite places to hold ceremonies. The different groups or nations spoke many different languages, but they traded with each other and had contact with each other, sometimes friendly, sometimes not. They invented many things, like digging sticks, woomeras (wooden spear-launchers) and boomerangs, which whirled through the air to kill an animal or bird and then came back to the owner. Some had permanent settlements where they built dwellings, made fish and animal traps and cultivated areas for food growing.

Aboriginal and Torres Strait Islander Australians have their own history, not set down in dates or writing, but stretching back over many thousands of years and told by generation after generation. Aboriginal people believe that their spirit ancestors made the land and the people. These 'creation spirits', such as the Rainbow Serpents, the Lightning Men, The Wagalag Sisters, the Tingari and Wandjina, were the source of all understanding, including the religious, ceremonial and social rules of kinship and marriage, and the laws of behaviour and punishment.

For the Aboriginal people the whole of Australia is covered by a web of dreamings, varying in particular places and regions and sometimes spreading across vast areas of country. The stories were passed down through the centuries, and were the basis of Aboriginal art stretching back over 50,000 years.

WANT TO KNOW MORE?

www.australianhistory.org/first-australians.

WANDJUK MARIKA was an elder of the Rirratjingu people of north-eastern Arnhem land. Mawalan, Wandjuk's father, taught him to paint. Wandjuk became both a successful artist and a cultural ambassador for his people. He was awarded an Order of the British Empire in 1979.

Wandjuk's painting depicts the Rirratjingu people's Creation Ancestors, the Djang' kawu brother and sisters, on the sacred beach at Yalangbara. Wandjuk was the custodian of the sacred beach.

In the Rirratjingu Creation knowledge the Djang'kawu brother and sisters travelled across Arnhem land, creating and naming all the animals and plants and natural features. They arrived at Yalangbara, carrying magical dilly bags, conical mats and digging sticks. The brother is standing at the top of the painting. With his digging sticks he had created waterholes and now the sticks will turn into the trees which stand beside him. His sisters, below him, have given birth to the first people. The different colours of the figures indicate the different clans. The changing pattern of the ground, the pattern of the Rirratjingu clan, represents the shifting sands of the beach at Yalangbara.

DID YOU KNOW?

The Aboriginal and Torres Strait Islander people of Australia are not one racial group, but many clans who are as different from each other in customs and appearance as are European people from many countries.

DID YOU KNOW?

The Aboriginal language in Australia is one of the most linguistically diverse in the world. There were between 200 and 250 aboriginal languages spoken, with many different dialects, producing up to 700 varieties.

2. The first Australians in danger

Benjamin Duterrau (1767–1851)
Mr Robinson's first interview with Timmy,
1840
Oil on canvas
113 x 142 cm
National Gallery of Australia

THE FIRST MEETINGS between the Europeans and Aboriginal people were tense, with the Aboriginal people completely mystified by these strange people. One group of Aborigines thought that the soldiers' red uniforms and fancy hats were part of their bodies, and were delighted when the soldiers stripped off to show that they were human.

Governor Arthur Phillip ordered the first Europeans to make friends with the local Aboriginal inhabitants. Despite the good intentions, however, there were violent incidents on both sides, and then hostility as the Europeans spread out, and the Aboriginal people realised that their

DUTERRAU PAINTED many pictures of Aborigines, sometimes including George Augustus Robinson.

In this image, Duterrau paints the light shining on Robinson, who is encouraging Timmy and his people to leave their traditional life. Timmy listens, one hand resting in Robinson's and one on the shoulder of his Aboriginal companion. For Duterrau and his contemporaries, Timmy's choice was clear. They thought that Robinson's protection would give the Tasmanian Aborigines a brighter future, but the removal from their traditional lands and life caused them distress and heartache.

Benjamin Duterrau worked as an engraver before achieving success as a portrait painter and landscape artist. In 1832, at the age of 65, he emigrated to Tasmania with his daughter. He became one of Australia's most important colonial artists.

traditional lands were being taken. Large numbers of the Aboriginal population also became sick and died from European diseases.

Over many decades there were skirmishes and battles as the Aboriginal people were subdued. Where the Europeans settled Aboriginal people were driven away. Only the people of the vast desert and scrub-lands of the centre and north were able to continue their traditional way of life.

The white dominance remains in Australia today, although there is a gradual acceptance that the Aboriginal people were wronged, particularly the 'stolen generation', children taken away from their parents and brought up in white society.

Aboriginal people all over Australia still feel pain and anger over their treatment by the early settlers, and also by later generations of white Australians and their governments. A renewal of co-operation and assistance was symbolised in the Australian Parliament on February 13, 2008, when Prime Minister Kevin Rudd delivered a formal apology to the Aboriginal people for the wrongs of the past.

Due to European diseases and conflict the Aboriginal people of Tasmania, who numbered about 5,000–10,000 before European settlement, were reduced to about 300 people some 30 years later. This remaining group fought tenaciously for their land. In 1830, Governor George Arthur lined up his troops and they marched the length of the island to round up any stragglers, but without much success.

In 1833, George Robinson was appointed 'Protector of Aborigines'. He convinced this remaining group, with promises of a better life, to cease hostilities with the settlers and move to Flinders Island in Bass Strait.

There, removed from their traditional lands most of them died. Fourteen years later, the remaining 47 were brought back to the mainland to a settlement at Oyster Cove. About a decade after this only about a dozen people remained and the last of this group, Trucaninni, died in 1876.

Benjamin Law (1807–1882)
Trucaninny, wife of Woureddy (Aboriginal Chief of Van Diemen's Land), 1836
Cast plaster, painted
66 x 42.5 x 25.7 cm
National Gallery of Australia

BENJAMIN LAW'S striking bust of Trucaninny is the earliest major piece of Australian sculpture. Trucaninny's mother and her first husband were killed by white settlers. Law's sympathetic sculpture depicts a woman grieving for her family members and for her race.

Benjamin Law was born in Sheffield, England, in 1807. He and his wife arrived in Hobart in 1835 as assisted agricultural emigrants. Despite his considerable talent, Law was not able to earn his living as a sculptor and worked at different times as a school-teacher, a storekeeper, and a postman. He died in Melbourne in 1882 aged 75.

IN THE PICTURE

The Aboriginal people of Tasmania often decorated their hair to make a kind of helmet of ochre coloured mud, as can be seen on the two background figures in the painting.

3. A fresh start in Australia

Abraham Solomon (1824–1862)
Second Class – the parting: 'Thus part we rich in sorrow parting poor', 1854
Oil on canvas
69.4 x 96.6 cm
National Gallery of Australia

IN *SECOND CLASS – the parting: 'Thus part we rich in sorrow parting poor'* a boy is saying goodbye to his family. He is travelling by train to an English seaport from where he will sail for Australia, the land of opportunity. His sister is in tears while his mother holds him tenderly. The painting was done in 1854 and the poster behind him is about Port Phillip and the gold rush. He is off to seek his fortune. During the reign of Queen Victoria (1837 to 1901) almost fifteen million people, known as emigrants, left the British Isles to settle in other countries. People fled the potato famine in Ireland, the land clearances in Scotland and the agricultural revolution in England.

Australia offered a fresh start for the men and women of Britain. In the early days of the colony they were mostly convicts or the soldiers who guarded them. The jails of England were shockingly overcrowded, and people were sentenced to transportation for such small crimes as stealing a loaf of bread.

Many convicts were left to 'rot in hell' in dreadful prisons around Sydney, on Norfolk Island and in Tasmania. Those who caused trouble might face the whip or death by hanging. Others who behaved well were granted their freedom, and some were given land. Land grants were also given to soldiers, especially the officers, and some created big farming properties.

Convict ships kept arriving for many decades, but there were also many free immigrants seeking new opportunities. Many single girls from poor families came out from England to find work, often as servants, and possibly to find a husband.

The biggest wave of immigrants in the 19th century came after news spread about the discovery of gold in New South Wales and Victoria in 1851. In a single year, Victoria's population doubled to 110,000.

A YOUNG boy is joining a ship to sail to Australia. The posters that attracted him are displayed on the carriage wall behind him. His widowed mother and sister are accompanying him on the train trip to the coast where the ship awaits. The quote in the title 'Thus part we rich in sorrow parting poor' is from Shakespeare's play *Timon of Athens*. It underlines the depth of the pain of the parting and the poverty which forces the young boy to seek his fortune so far away. The artist uses dark colours to convey the sadness felt by the boy's family. However the sunlit harbour, glimpsed through the window of the train, suggests a brighter future for the young man.

Abraham Solomon began studying art at the age of 13. He showed such talent that he gained entry into London's famous Royal Academy of Art at the age of 16. He painted romantic and dramatic works for the popular market. His English audience loved a picture that told a story. His *Second Class – the parting: 'Thus part we rich in sorrow parting poor'* was a companion work to the scandalous *First class - the meeting* in which a young man flirts with a girl in a railway carriage while her father sleeps. Abraham Solomon died at the age of 38, at the height of his fame.

IN THE PICTURE

Abraham Solomon used extreme skill and patience to convey a lot of details in the picture, with information about Port Phillip and Sydney and a WANTED poster using the British Coat of Arms.

DID YOU KNOW?

Michael Solomon, the artist's father, was a hat maker in London and was the first person of Jewish descent to be given the Freedom of the City of London. Abraham Solomon's sister Rebecca and brother Simeon were also successful artists.

WANT TO KNOW MORE?

www.museumvictoria.com.au/immigrationmuseum/

4. Why our animals are different

John Wolseley's picture *Botanist's camp: tropical night* is about the unique animal, bird and plant world of Australia. When the lands of Asia and Australia were further apart, many thousands of years ago, the birds and animals were naturally divided between the tropical and temperate areas of the world.

The gap between the lands has closed, but there is a narrow passage in the ocean, with quite different sorts of animals and birds on either side.

John Wolseley (1938–)
Botanist's camp, tropical night, 1997
Lithograph
74 x 93.5 cm
National Gallery of Australia

Mickey of Ulladulla (c.1820–1891)
Untitled. Fishing, native fauna, c 1888
Pencil, gouache, watercolour
43 x 68 cm
National Gallery of Australia

This gap was discovered by Alfred Russel Wallace in 1859, and is known as the Wallace Line. It runs north of Bali and south of Lombok in Indonesia and travels to the south of the Philippines.

On the northern side are monkeys, tigers, elephants, bears, deer and antelope, and Asian birds such as trogans and barbets. On the southern side are the marsupial species—kangaroos and wallabies, wombats and koalas—and the monotremes, the echidna and the platypus. Among the southern species of birds are emus and cassowaries, parrots and honeyeaters, galahs and cockatoos, kookaburras and magpies.

We also know that Australia once had megafauna, such as gigantic kangaroos, wombats as big as hippopotami, huge snakes and lizards, and a ferocious marsupial 'lion'. They became extinct about 20,000 years ago. It is thought that the megafauna's disappearance is linked to the arrival of Aboriginal people. Their use of fire changed the landscape, so there was no longer enough vegetation for the megafauna to eat.

MICKEY'S PICTURE records the fish, birds and animals living in his area. Birds are sitting in trees, kangaroos lie in the grass and men are fishing from a boat. The peacocks and a horse, introduced by white settlers, are surrounded by native animals and birds.

Mickey of Ulladulla is one of the few Aboriginal artists of the 19th century whose works have survived. Some of Mickey's first drawings, held in the Mitchell Library, Sydney, bear the note: "Drawn by 'Mickie', an old crippled blackfellow of Nellingen, Clyde River, NSW, 1875."

Ulladulla is a fishing and timber port on the NSW south coast. Many Aboriginal people in the area were employed by white settlers in such things as forest clearing, saw-milling, farming and fishing. Mickey's drawings record these activities as well as traditional corroborees and ceremonies. In many of his paintings a black man in European dress is seen supporting himself on crutches. This man is thought to be Mickey himself. After his death, five of his drawings were shown at the Chicago World Exposition.

WHY DON'T YOU?

Make a drawing of some of the wild birds and animals that live near you.

THE PICTURE, *Botanist's camp: tropical night*, places in the foreground the botanist's detailed drawings and notes. The colourful collection of animals and plants dominates the picture. Man intrudes in the form of a GPS (Global Positioning System) receiver with which the botanist records the exact position of each plant. In the background the tent, evidence of man's temporary presence, hovers above the land. The human visitors will leave no lasting imprint on the landscape.

John Wolseley studied art in his country of birth, England. He worked in France and Spain and was already an internationally renowned artist when he arrived in Australia in 1976. Every year John Wolseley spends many months working and painting in the Australian bush. His art reflects his love of the land, how the land changes, and how people adapt to the natural environment.

John Wolseley often brings natural things into his pictures, tracing lines with burned wood and sticking leaves, feathers and dead insects on to his pictures.

5. The mad rush for gold

S. T. Gill (1818–1880)
Cradling, Forest Creek, 1852
Lithograph
15.2 x 20.6 cm
National Gallery of Australia

GOLD PUT AUSTRALIA on the world map. Adventurers rushed to the diggings in sailing ships from Europe, America and Asia. There were so many ships arriving at the port of Melbourne, 150 kilometres from the Ballarat gold fields, that it was described as being 'a forest of masts'.

Finding gold was mostly a matter of luck, and many miners failed after years of work. They were left without shelter and food, and with little hope.

The first gold was found near Bathurst in New South Wales in 1851, but the central Victorian gold fields proved to be the richest. The scenes on the gold fields were amazing, with tents and huts everywhere and people digging frantically. They would dig up the soil and wash off the 'pay-dirt'

SAMUEL GILL'S art has a human quality and shows the excitement and drama of life on the crowded goldfields. In *Cradling, Forest Creek*, two diggers are using a small box, shaped like a cradle, to wash the earth away from the gold. The diggers on Forest Creek had to pay for water and when water was scarce, cradling had to stop. The artist created this print by drawing on a smooth stone with a waxy pencil. This type of print is called a lithograph.

Samuel Thomas Gill arrived in South Australia from England in 1839. His father, a clergyman and amateur artist, had taught him to draw. Gill sketched scenes of Adelaide and published them in a collection entitled *South Australia Illustrated*. In 1846 he travelled beyond the Flinders Ranges with the explorer John Horrocks, an expedition in which Horrocks was fatally wounded and his companions suffered great hardship.

In 1851 he joined hopeful prospectors in the Victorian goldfields. His drawings captured every aspect of the colourful life on the goldfields and were published in his book *Sketches of the Victorian Gold Diggings and Diggers As They Are*, which sold well both in Australia and England.

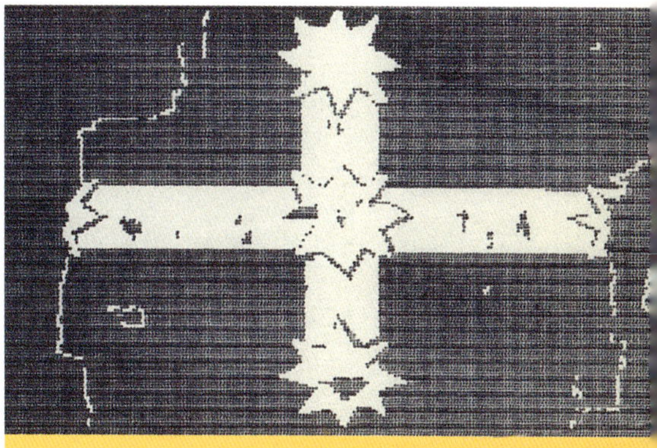

William Kelly (1943–)
Still life: Eureka flag, 1981
Dot matrix computer generated print
5.6 x 9.8 cm
National Gallery of Australia

with water to see if there were any specks or grains of gold.

In the early days, nuggets of gold were found near the surface, but this easy gold soon ran out. The long-lasting wealth came from deeper seams of gold, dug out over many years by mining companies.

The hardship of the early miners' lives is depicted by the gold field artist S.T. Gill in *Cradling, Forest Creek*. In Victoria the miners soon began to complain bitterly about the exorbitant licence fee of thirty shillings a month. The Ballarat miners declared they would not pay this tax.

They built a wooden fort called the Eureka Stockade for protection against the armed government troops that were sent from Melbourne. The miners swore allegiance to their newly created flag, the Southern Cross.

The rebellion came to a bloody ending on 3 December 1854 when government troops charged the stockade, shooting at the miners. In a short battle twenty-four miners were killed and many more were wounded. Their leaders were put on trial, but all were acquitted, and one, Peter Lalor, later became a Member of Parliament. The battle of Eureka is now held to be a triumph for the working people against an oppressive and undemocratic government. The flag of the Southern Cross, depicted in William Kelly's *Eureka Flag*, is still seen at many a trade union rally.

STILL LIFE: *Eureka Flag* is simple and evocative. Kelly used a computer to produce a strikingly realistic image of the tattered remains of the original Eureka flag. The Eureka flag was raised by gold-miners during the 1854 rebellion at Eureka Stockade. Peter Lalor, leader of the Ballarat Reform League, stood beneath this flag and swore to defend the gold-miners' rights and liberties. The flag's silver cross and stars represent the Southern Cross, a constellation visible only in the southern hemisphere.

William Kelly was born in the United States of America. At the age of 17 he saw Giorgio de Chirico's 'simple, poetic, and evocative' *The Anguish of the Departure*. He decided to become an artist. Kelly attended the University of the Arts in Philadelphia. He came to Australia on a Fulbright scholarship and continued his studies at the National Gallery School in Melbourne. He is a painter, a teacher and lover of drawing, and a printmaker. He has organised and participated in collaborative art projects. His 1993 installation, entitled 'Peace project', earned him the Australian Violence Prevention Award.

DID YOU KNOW?

There were five main manual methods of finding gold used by the early miners: Panning – swishing dirt round in a pan, with the heavier gold sinking to the bottom; cradling – similar to panning, but with much more dirt and water; dry blowing – (used in dry conditions) dropping dirt from one pan to the other with the idea that the dust would blow away, leaving the gold; puddling – separating gold from clay by dumping clay in a container, filling it with water and then stirring with a paddle; shafting – digging in the ground with a pick and shovel.

WANT TO KNOW MORE?

www.sovereignhill.com.au

6. Bushfires, the scourge of summer

William Strutt (1825–1915)
Black Thursday, Melbourne, Victoria 1851
(c. 1863)
Pencil, watercolour and wash on paper.
14.1 x 25 cm
National Gallery of Australia

THE SMOKE, the heat, the noise and the smell of bushfires are fearful experiences of Australia's summers. One of the worst fires was in Victoria in 1851, and the terror of it is captured in William Strutt's picture *Black Thursday, Melbourne, Victoria.*

Before European settlement bushfires were usually caused by lightning

A DEVASTATING bushfire swept through Victoria in February 1851. William Strutt talked to eyewitnesses and made many sketches. This sketch captures what he described as 'a stampede for life'. Back in England several sketches, including this one, formed the basis for a large painting which is considered to be his finest.

William Strutt was born in England. Both his father and grandfather were artists. After studying art in Paris he was soon very busy providing illustrations for magazines and books. A heavy work-load and deteriorating eye-sight led him to leave London for Melbourne.

The change was refreshing but he was soon hard at work again, with commissioned portraits, illustrations, and designs for stamps, posters and maps. He lived in New Zealand for four years, producing many fine paintings of landscapes and Maori groups. He returned to England in 1862, at the age of 37.

strikes, or by the Aboriginal tradition of burning to speed up the growth of food plants. These days they are likely to be caused by carelessness, such as dropped cigarettes and people lighting barbecue fires in the bush, or by sparks from machinery. Hot, windy days in summer are declared Total Fire Ban days. Some fires are deliberately lit by arsonists or firebugs, who face severe penalties if they are caught.

William Strutt's picture was of the first big fire recorded in Victoria. Its worst day became known as Black Thursday, on 6 February 1851, when fires burned a quarter of the state. There was another devastating fire in 1898 and the worst day of all, known as Black Friday, came on 6 January 1939, when the fires roared through the south-eastern forests, killing 71 people. The horror and waste of it led to the Country Fire Authority, with its volunteer fire fighters, being set up.

Among the worst fires of more recent times were the Ash Wednesday fires on 13 February 1983, when 47 people died and around 2,000 houses were lost, and the firestorms which hit the national capital, Canberra, on 18 January 2003. In January 2007 huge fires raged for more than a month in the forests of north-eastern Victoria, and fire-fighters saved many threatened towns and homes.

DID YOU KNOW?

Bushfires in Australia spread as a thin front of flame, with flames usually about as thick as they are high. Forest fires normally travel at one to three km/h, have flames 10–20 metres high and thick, and will pass a spot in 30–60 seconds. Severe forest fires travel at up to 12 km/h, with flames 100–150 metres high and thick. Grass fires generally travel about three to ten km/h, but speeds of around 25 km/h have been recorded.

Fred Williams (1927–1982)
Burnt landscape II, 1968
Watercolour, gouache, clay, charcoal
56.8 x 76.6 cm
National Gallery of Australia

A FOREST of trees on a hill-top has been reduced to sparse, blackened trunks. Some trunks are just vertical lines; others are contorted and misshapen. The fire has replaced the colours of life with browns, reds, greys, whites, and blacks. Burnt debris seems to be floating above the devastation. *Burnt landscape II* shows Fred Williams's abstract, minimalist and yet powerful style.

Fred Williams was born in Melbourne. He studied at the National Gallery Art School and at George Bell's private school. In the 1950s he travelled to Europe where he continued his studies and learned etching and printing techniques. When he returned to Australia he began working on landscapes. Williams referred to himself as a 'painter/etcher'. He won the Wynne Prize for landscape painting in 1966 and 1976.

7. The wide land under water

Noël Nicolson (1937–)
Flash flood, 1992
Lithograph
38.5 x 28.2 cm
National Gallery of Australia

AUSTRALIA IS THE world's driest continent, but it cannot escape from floods. The inland plains of eastern Australia carry a vast network of rivers known as the Murray-Darling Basin. When heavy rain occurs in the basin, which stretches from Queensland down into Victoria, these inland rivers can burst their banks. Noël Nicolson's *Flash Flood* shows the beginnings of disaster as a river bursts its banks.

In the time of the riverboat trade, from the 1860s to the 1920s, floods allowed the flat-bottomed paddle steamers on the Murray-Darling system to travel far away from the rivers to pick up cargo. They would be seen paddling away on what was usually dry and dusty land.

In a more fierce kind of flooding, heavy rainfall near the east coast can turn coastal rivers into raging torrents. 'Flash floods' like these caused havoc in Brisbane in 1893 and Melbourne in 1930. The Brisbane downpour of 1318 millimetres in a day submerged part of the city centre and 17 riverside suburbs.

The annual 'wet' in the tropical north, between November and March, floods parts of the inland. The overflowing of the northern rivers creates the beautiful wetlands of Kakadu each year, and provides water for irrigated farm-lands around the Ord River and other areas of the north. Over many thousands of years these floodwaters have worn away the landscape to create famous features, like Katherine Gorge in the Northern Territory and the honeycomb mountains of Purnululu in the Kimberley region of Western Australia.

The most tragic Australian flood was at Gundagai, New South Wales, in 1844. The Murrumbidgee River burst its banks one night and inundated the houses of settlers. People climbed on to roofs or into gum trees, but 87 people died. Today's Gundagai is built on the hills above the flood plain, which is crossed by a bridge on the Hume Highway. In June 2007 huge floods hit the Hunter Valley of New South Wales, killing seven people and destroying homes, roads and farmland, and in 2008 flooding was widespread in Queensland.

FLASH FLOOD captures the flooding of the Yarra Valley after sudden, torrential rain. The elemental force is unrelenting. The Yarra River has broken its banks and is racing and swirling across the land, creating new rivers and lakes. Trees struggle to stand upright. Roads will be cut off and homes isolated until the water recedes just as quickly as it rose. Irrigation, dams, and less rainfall have made the flash flood in this area an event of the past.

Noël Nicolson was born in London. A year later her family moved to Australia, settling in Melbourne. Nicolson studied art at the Royal Melbourne Institute of Technology and became an art teacher. She is a painter and printmaker.

In the early 1960s Nicolson and her husband moved to a family farm in the Yarra Valley. The homestead (owned by artists Arthur and Minnie Boyd at the beginning of the 20th century) sits on a bank of the Yarra River, which meanders leisurely through a flood plain.

DID YOU KNOW?

A University of South Australia Research team discovered, by studying the spread of the Black Box Tree, that there had been a flood on the River Murray around the year 1750 that had reached a level 2.11 metres higher than the greatest recorded river height in 1956 of 15.9 metres above sea level. The team was able to determine that such a flood will occur once in every 1000 years, but not the actual decade or even century when that might happen.

8. The sad ending of Burke and Wills

Nicholas Chevalier (1828–1902)
Return of Burke and Wills to Coopers Creek, 1873–1876
Engraving
11.9 x 18 cm
National Gallery of Australia

THE ORDEAL OF the explorers Burke and Wills reached its climax in the loneliness and heat of Central Australia. In the engraving *Return of Burke and Wills to Coopers Creek* the explorers, with William King, struggle desperately back to the depot at Cooper's Creek where they expect a base party to be waiting for them.

Burke and Wills's journey in 1860–61 was one of the last great feats of exploration. Most of eastern Australia was known by then, but the inland country from the centre to the north was the last big puzzle. Was it farming land or desert, forests or swamps?

Robert O'Hara Burke and William John Wills started from Melbourne, but they made their dash for the north coast from Cooper's Creek in the centre. They took Charles Gray and William King, camels and horses, and they left other men behind to wait for their return.

After slogging across deserts, plains and swamps, they made it to the northern coast at the Gulf of Carpentaria. They did not reach the sea, but they saw the tidal waters in the mangrove thickets that stopped them. Getting back was worse. They were exhausted, starved and getting slower and slower. Charles Gray died before they staggered back into camp. The base party had left just that morning, after waiting for 96 days. They left some food buried in the ground under a tree with the word cut in the bark—DIG.

Burke, Wills and King were too weak to follow them, but later tried to reach a police post at Mt Hopeless in South Australia. Lack of water forced them to turn back, and they slowly starved in the Cooper's Creek area.

Only William King, with help from the local Aboriginals, survived to tell the tragic tale. The funeral procession of Burke and Wills in 1852 was watched by 40,000 mourners, the largest crowd assembled in Australia to that time.

DID YOU KNOW?

John O'Hara Burke sacked his original second in command before appointing the young surveyor William John Wills to the job. The first man was Lieutenant George Landells, who had brought the expedition camels from India. Burke was outraged to find that Landells was giving the camels whisky in their drinking water.

IN 1860 Burke and Wills led an expedition to cross Australia from south to north. They successfully reached the Gulf of Carpentaria. However, the expedition is remembered more for the tragic ending. This print depicts Burke, Wills and King on the fateful return to Cooper's Creek.

Nicholas Chevalier's mother was Russian and his father Swiss. He studied art in Switzerland, England and Italy. In 1854 he travelled to Australia and was soon employed as an artist and illustrator. Chevalier was the official artist on Professor Neumayer's geological tour around Victoria in 1862. In 1864 his painting, *The Buffalo Range, Victoria*, was the first Australian work purchased by the newly founded National Gallery of Victoria.

In 1867 Australians were proud to receive their first royal visitor, Prince Alfred, Duke of Edinburgh. Chevalier travelled with the Duke's party during its tour of Victoria. The Duke was impressed by Chevalier's artistic, musical and linguistic talents and invited him and his family to accompany the royal party on its journey back to England. In England Chevalier continued to enjoy success. He died in London in 1902.

WANT TO KNOW MORE?

www. burkeandwills.net.au

9. Australia on the sheep's back

THE FIRST VALUABLE commodity in Australia was wool. By the 1790s Captain John McArthur had begun experimenting with sheep breeding for wool at his property, Elizabeth Farm, Parramatta.

Soon pioneer settlers claimed vast areas for sheep runs to supply wool for the factories of England. They were known as 'squatters', as originally they did not buy the land, but simply 'squatted' on it, claiming it as their own. They became the wealthiest class of people in Australia, building fine mansions and employing many people on their properties.

George Lambert's painting *Weighing the fleece* has the wool as its

George Lambert (1873–1930)
Weighing the fleece, 1921
Oil on canvas
71.7 x 91.8 cm
National Gallery of Australia

WEIGHING THE FLEECE was commissioned by the wealthy pastoralist, F.S. Falkiner of Wanganella in the Riverina region of New South Wales. The focus of the painting, and the source of the pastoralist's wealth, is the white fleece from the champion merino. It will fetch a record price. With a haughty eye Falkiner watches his nephew weighing the fleece. His wife sits apart, her back resting on a bale of the wool.

The scene takes place in the shearing shed, a quintessential image of Australian life. Lambert was proud of his attention to detail – like the timber beams, the swallow droppings, the corrugated iron, the oil drum, the kerosene tin.

George Lambert's widowed mother brought him from England to Australia at the age of 14. He spent the first eight months living on his great-uncle's sheep station in New South Wales. He fell in love with country life.

He studied art in Sydney and became an illustrator for the *The Bulletin* magazine, before returning to England on an art scholarship. During World War 1 Lambert went to Palestine as an official war artist.

focus, emphasising the size and importance of the wool industry to the Australian economy.

The industry today follows the patterns of the past, when gangs of shearers went from property to property for the annual shearing, taking their own cooks and shed hands with them. The fastest shearers were called 'guns' and there was a race in each shed for the highest daily tallies.

The greatest 'gun' with hand shears was Jacky Howe, who sheared a record 327 merino sheep in one eight-hour day at Alice Downs, Queensland, in 1892. Today's machine shearing record was set in 2007 by Darin Forde, with 721 sheep shorn in nine hours in New Zealand.

The Great Shearers' Strike of 1891 was caused when Queensland landowners tried to lower the shearers' prices. The shearers assembled at the town of Barcaldine in protest and formed the Shearers' Union. Government troops soon arrived, and after a short affray 12 strike leaders were arrested and jailed. The strikers eventually won, in one of the first examples of industrial action in Australia, and the shearers' strike led to the foundation of the Australian Labor Party.

Wool hit the heights in the 1950s during the Korean War, when it sold at a rate of $37 per kilo. A popular saying was that Australia was 'riding on the sheep's back'. Even with the decline in value caused by the development of synthetic fibres, Australia's wool clip was still worth $3.5 billion in the year 2005.

Jeff Carter (1928–)
Pure merinos, Sydney sheep show, 1961
Photograph
24 x 37.3 cm
National Gallery of Australia

JEFF CARTER makes an ironic statement when the then Prime Minister of Australia, Robert Menzies, a member of the noble breed of the Australian Establishment, looks at prize rams at the 1961 Sydney sheep show.

In 1946 Jeff Carter began travelling around Australia with his camera and typewriter, selling his stories and photographs to Australian and overseas newspapers and magazines. To supplement a hard-earned income he worked at odd jobs. He was a drover, a fruit picker, a road worker and a mill hand.

Carter admired the strength and the endurance shown by Australians working in tough environments. He took many photographs of agricultural shows, markets, circuses and travelling shows. His photographs are a remarkable record of Australian life, and his many books include *People of the Inland* (1966) and *Stout Hearts and Leathery Hands* (1967). He produced and filmed a television series, *Wild Country*. His works are held in many collections and especially at the National Library of Australia.

DID YOU KNOW?

Australia is the world's largest producer of wool, and its largest customer is China, even though China has more sheep. More than 80 per cent of Australia's sheep are merinos, noted for the super-fine wool. More than a third of our wool is grown in New South Wales.

WANT TO KNOW MORE

www. woolinnovation.com.au

10. The style of the cities

Tom Roberts (1856–1931)
Allegro con brio, Bourke Street west,
c.1885–86, additions 1890
Oil on canvas, mounted on
composition board
51.2 x 76.7 cm
National Gallery of Australia and the
National Library of Australia

BEFORE 1851 THE Governor in Sydney controlled all the Australian colonies, sending his decisions to the outpost cities of Hobart and Melbourne, Brisbane and Adelaide. When Victoria was granted independence as a separate colony in 1850, posters were put up around Melbourne, saying: 'Glorious News—Free at Last'.

Tom Robert's 1880s painting *Allegro con brio, Bourke Street west* captures the bustle of Bourke Street, Melbourne on a hot summer's day.

The population of Melbourne was then around 400,000 people.

Greater Melbourne today has a population approaching four million people.

Settlement at Hobart began in 1804, at Brisbane in 1826 and Perth in 1829. Melbourne did not start up until 1835 and Adelaide not until 1836. Each began differently. Hobart and Brisbane were both convict colonies, set up from the original convict settlement in Sydney, while the free settlers in Perth and Adelaide came straight from England. John Batman founded Melbourne when he sailed across from Tasmania, 'bought' the land with gifts to the Aboriginal people of the area, and chose an area along the Yarra River for settlement.

The colonial capitals each grew in their own way. Sydney's narrow city streets follow the pathways and lanes of the first settlement, while Hobart sits snugly between its waterfront and Mt Wellington. Brisbane's plan is complicated by the twists and turns of the Brisbane River, while Melbourne's wide city streets and narrow lanes form a grid pattern established by the surveyor Robert Hoddle. Adelaide's surveyor, William Light, designed his inner city around squares and surrounded them with parkland. In each city the buildings followed the English styles of the times, but deep and shady verandas were usually added to ward off the fierce Australian heat.

TOM ROBERTS'S painting of Bourke Street in Melbourne was inspired by French artist Claude Monet's bird's eye views of Parisian streets. 'Allegro con brio' is a musical term which tells the musicians to play moderately quickly and with spirit.

Roberts selected a high viewpoint by the post office to paint the hustle and bustle of Bourke Street, in the full glare of the sun, looking west into William Street. His chosen view to the rise of the Bourke Street hill allowed him to paint the full length of the busy street, the waiting cabs, the offices and shops and the welcome patches of shade under awnings and verandas.

Tom Roberts was born in England. When his father died in 1868 his mother took the family to Australia to join relatives in Melbourne. Roberts enrolled in the National Gallery School, Melbourne, in 1874, but returned to England to study in 1881. Back in Australia in 1885 he established an artists' camp at Box Hill, Victoria. These artists became known as the Heidelberg School and were Australia's impressionist painters. After his death Roberts was acknowledged as the father of Australian landscape painting.

Lloyd Rees (1895–1988)
The Summit, Ball's Head, 1978
Etching
25.0 x 30.4 cm
National Gallery of Australia

THE SUMMIT, Ball's Head is a view of Lloyd Rees's favourite stretch of water (Sydney Harbour) and his favourite city (Sydney). Beyond the rocks and vegetation, beyond the ferries and the boats, beyond the houses and the spires, appear the multi-storey, concrete and glass office blocks and the ever-present cranes, busily erecting more. Rees thought modern, functional architecture was dehumanising. He loved Sydney but rejoiced at the restoration of streets and corners of the 'old' Sydney he had grown to love in the early decades of the 20th century.

Lloyd Rees was born in Brisbane and studied art at Brisbane Technical College. He worked for the Queensland Printing Office and then an advertising firm in Sydney, all the time drawing and painting and studying art. Four trips to Europe further developed his technique and his style. Rees became a respected landscape painter. He won the Wynne prize for his landscapes in 1950 and 1982. He was in his eighties when he turned to printmaking. In those later years his failing eyesight may have been a factor in his style moving from realism to abstraction.

11. Ned Kelly goes down fighting

Sidney Nolan (1917–1992)
The trial, 1947
Enamel on composition board
90.4 x 121.2 cm
National Gallery of Australia

NED KELLY WAS the leader of a gang of bushrangers in Victoria in the 1880s. Sidney Nolan's *The trial* is part of a series of paintings that tell the Kelly story. In the paintings the square topped helmet of Kelly's armour has become a symbol of the man himself.

Ned's life did not start too well. His father was transported to Australia

from Ireland for stealing pigs. Ned was born at Beveridge, Victoria, in 1854. When he was 12 his father died and he had to leave school to help support his family. Ned's widowed mother moved her eight children to a slab hut near Greta in northern Victoria.

Despite his poverty-stricken upbringing, Ned was tall, strong and handsome. He was an expert horseman, a champion boxer, and a deadly accurate shot. As a schoolboy he had won an award for rescuing seven-year-old Richard Shelton from drowning in a flooded river.

Ned and his brother Dan were soon in trouble with the police, accused of petty theft and horse stealing. They took to the bush with two other young men, Joe Byrne and Ben Hart, leaving their hideouts to hold up travellers or rob banks.

The four men in Kelly's gang were among the last of Australia's bushrangers. Most of the bushrangers were escaped convicts, but some were just attracted to the wild life. Among the most famous were Ben Hall, 'Bold' Jack Donohue, 'Captain Moonlight' (Andrew Scott), 'Thunderbolt' (Fred Ward) and 'Mad Dan' Morgan.

After one robbery at Jerilderie, New South Wales, Ned Kelly wrote a long letter claiming he had been badly treated by police all his life. The gang were seen by some as heroes, but they were soon 'WANTED, DEAD OR ALIVE' after they killed three policemen who found their hideout.

Becoming bold and desperate, they robbed the bank at the tiny town of Euroa, Victoria. They held all the people in the town captive and showed off with exhibitions of trick riding. They then rode to the nearby town of Glenrowan and herded all the citizens into the hotel, while they waited for a shoot-out with police.

During a wild night of shooting Ned escaped from the hotel and put on armour he had made from scrap metal. He came striding through the bush in the early morning, firing at the police, but they brought him down with shots to his legs. 'I am done', he said. Inside the hotel the three other bushrangers, including his brother Dan, were dead.

At Ned Kelly's trial in Melbourne he argued with the judge, Sir Redmond Barry. In 1878, at Beechworth, Barry had sentenced Ned's mother to three years of hard labour on false and unsubstantiated evidence. When he sentenced Kelly to death by hanging, Barry uttered the customary words, 'May God have mercy on your soul'. Kelly replied: 'I will go a little further than that, and say I will see you there when I go.'

Ned Kelly was hanged at the Old Melbourne Jail on 11 November 1880. His last words were, 'Such is life'. Twelve days later Sir Redmond Barry died.

STANDING PROUDLY in the middle of the courtroom Ned Kelly towers over the sickly judge, the small green-faced policeman and the distant jury. Kelly's dominating presence shows Nolan's belief in the heroic status of the famous bushranger.

Sidney Nolan was born in Melbourne. From the age of 17 to 21 he worked in the art department of a hat factory and attended evening classes at the National Gallery School. His paintings attracted the attention of critics and wealthy art patrons.

Nolan painted his 'Kelly' series in 1946 and 1947. He said 'The Kelly paintings are secretly about myself. It's an inner history of my own emotions, but I am not going to tell you about them.' Nolan's grandfather, William Nolan, had been a Victorian police sergeant chasing the Kellys at Beechworth and told stories of how the police did their best to avoid meeting with the bushrangers.

Nolan's 27 paintings depicting the life and trial of the bushranger are powerfully painted in simple, bright colours. The starkly simplified image of Kelly, in a square topped helmet, is one of the most familiar symbols in Australian art.

DID YOU KNOW

Sidney Nolan produced other series beside his Ned Kelly works. The subjects included the Burke and Wills story, the Eliza Fraser story, Gallipoli and the Anzacs, and Australia's 'dead heart', as seen from the air.

DID YOU KNOW?

The world's first full-length feature film, made in 1906, was the Australian production *The Story of the Kelly Gang*. Other well known films about Ned Kelly include: *Ned Kelly* (1970) starring English rock singer Mick Jagger; the *Trial of Ned Kelly* (1977); the 1980 mini-series *The Last Outlaw* and the 2003 *Ned Kelly*, which starred Heath Ledger.

12. Rabbits overrun the country

FOR MORE THAN a hundred years the humble rabbit, or billions of humble rabbits, overran Australia and turned much of the farming land into useless dirt. Rabbits breed at an alarming rate, a single female producing 48 little bunnies a year, each of which is ready to start their own breeding cycle after sixteen weeks.

Thomas Austin started the troubles in 1859, when he asked his nephew in England to send him 24 grey rabbits, five hares, 72 partridges and some sparrows so that he could continue his hobby of hunting in Australia. He released the animals and birds on his property *Barwon Park*, near Winchelsea, Victoria. He got plenty of rabbit meat for the table, but did not realise that the rabbits were spreading over the hills and far away.

Within ten years, the original 24 rabbits had multiplied so much that two million could be shot or trapped annually without having any noticeable effect on the population.

The farmers thought there was plenty of room for the rabbits alongside the sheep. It was not long, however, before they began to see bare paddocks and rabbits, rabbits everywhere. Many methods to get rid of them were tried—shooting, digging, netting, poisoning, setting dogs and ferrets on to them and using a machine, The Patent Rabbit Extractor.

One spectacular method was the rabbit drive, in which people would spread out and herd the rabbits into an ever-decreasing space.

The famous rabbit-proof fence was built between 1901 and 1907 in Western Australia, stretching for 1834 kilometres between the north west and the southern coasts, to try to keep the rabbits from spreading westwards. The fence held up their progress for some years, but a few got through and eventually two more fences took the length of construction past 3000 kilometres, again without stopping the rabbits.

The next solution, in 1951, was a scientific one, in which a disease called myxomatosis was introduced to spread from rabbit to rabbit by mosquito, causing them to become sick and die. The disease was 'engineered' so that it did not affect other animals or plants.

For a while the rabbits were virtually eradicated, but over the decades the survivors became immune to the disease and numbers grew again.

Another disease called calicivirus was released in 1996, but it was not as successful as myxomatosis. Rabbit numbers are down, but they are fighting back.

Sam Byrne (1883–1978)
Rabbit plague round-up into old mine,
c. 1962
Oil on composition board
60.0 x 61.4 cm
National Gallery of Australia

IN THIS painting Sam Byrne vividly recalls one of the many ways rabbits were exterminated during the rabbit plague of the early 20th century. Men on horseback are herding hundreds of rabbits into a disused mine-shaft. On the top of a tailings dump an Afghan camel rider looks down on the violent scene below.

Sam Byrne single-handedly chronicled the folk-history of Broken Hill over eight decades. He was born in 1883, the same year as the fabulous silver lode was discovered. He lived in the outback community of the Barrier Ranges, working as an underground miner and surface engine driver.

He began painting at the age of 66 and was still painting only weeks before he died in his 95th year. He painted small works in a naïve style, capturing local events such as sporting events, pub life, mining strikes, and an attack on a picnic train by two Afghans sympathetic to the Turkish cause during World War 1.

He painted in an old tin shed behind his home. He said:' It gave me great pleasure to accomplish something that would give fame after a life of hard work in the mine.'

DID YOU KNOW?

In 1926 there were an estimated 10 billion rabbits in Australia. It was the fastest spread recorded of any mammal in the world.

13. Mud, sweat and slow-moving wheels

WOOL DRAYS BY S.T. Gill shows the hardships of pioneering life and the difficulties of transport on the rough roads and trackless wastes of Australia.

In the early days, wagons pulled by teams of horses or bullocks carried goods around the country. The teams of bullocks, slow and steady, did most of the long hauls. They were whipped and cursed along the road by their drivers, known as 'bullockies'.

Many inland regions of eastern Australia were taken up by big landholders in the early 1800s, and then smallholding farmers during the latter half of the century. Wool was transported to railway sidings and ports on drays or carts pulled by teams of bullocks.

When winter rains turned the farmlands into muddy quagmires, it was

S.T. Gill (1818–1880)
Wool drays, 1865
Coloured lithograph
17.6 x 25.4 cm
National Gallery of Australia

J. W. Lindt (1845–1926)
Ferntree Gully, bullock dray, One Tree Hill,
c.1880–94
Photograph
15.0 x 20.0 cm
National Gallery of Australia

not unusual for wagons to founder in the deep mud, or even for teams to sink to a point of immobility. In summer the heat, the hard roads and rough terrain took their toll. Gill's picture has a bullock team straining against the yoke as it pulls a fully laden cart down a difficult slope.

Cobb & Co coaches, which began to operate in 1853, soon developed a passenger and parcel network on improved roads. Some coaches, such as *The Leviathan* on the Geelong–Ballarat run, could carry up to a 100 passengers. The spread of railways across Australia through the last twenty years of the century meant that horse and bullock wagons became an historical memory.

IN THE early days, wool was transported to railway sidings and ports on drays or carts pulled by teams of bullocks. The dray in the foreground is piled high with bales of wool, each one weighing about 120kg. A kettle and kerosene lamps hang from the dray. The bullocky is cracking his whip to urge on his team of eight strong bullocks as they make a difficult turn down a sloping track.

S.T. Gill was familiar with the hardships of life experienced by Australians in the country. He joined, as draftsman, the 1846 expedition led by John Horrocks to explore the land lying beyond Spencer Gulf, north of Adelaide. Members of the expedition lived under the stars and on short rations for four months. When Horrocks suffered a fatal gunshot wound Gill nursed him devotedly through his last weeks.

Gill later lived a rough life with the miners on the Victorian goldfields and travelled the countryside sketching authentic scenes which were later published in commercially successful books.

ONE TREE Hill stands at the top of the range that is now part of the Dandenong Ranges National Park.

A bullock team, such as the one in Lindt's photograph, could cover 30 kilometres a day. The biggest teams, with 27 bullocks, could move 100 bales of wool, a weight of about 14 tonnes.

John William Lindt was born in Germany in 1845, six years after the invention of the photograph. When he died, in 1926, he was an internationally famous master of a miraculous, nineteenth century invention.

Lindt ran away to sea, 'jumping ship' in Australia in 1863. He made a meagre living as a piano tuner before working as an apprentice to Conrad Wagner, an artist and photographer in Grafton. Lindt married Wagner's daughter and a few years later bought his father-in-law's business. In the 1870s he published his photographs of the Clarence River district and its Aboriginal people. He moved to Melbourne where his reputation as a photographer grew. In 1880 he photographed the capture of the Kelly gang at Glenrowan. Lindt loved the Australian bush. In 1895 he moved to the Hermitage, a house he had built at Blacks' Spur, near Mount Dom Dom. Surrounded by giant mountain ash and tree ferns, Lindt created an exotic garden which was designed by the famous botanist Ferdinand von Mueller. Lindt continued to work into his old age.

DID YOU KNOW?

The usual team consisted of 8 to 10 bullocks yoked side by side to a central pole. These powerful animals (the 'leaders', the 'polers' and the wild ones 'inside scrubbers') were difficult to control. The bullocky had skills that took many years to acquire. The whip was an essential tool, but all believed an extensive vocabulary of swear words was also required.

14. Messages along the singing wire

Clarice Beckett (1887 – 1935)
Road with telegraph poles, c.1932
Oil on cardboard
23.7 x 18.8 cm
National Gallery of Australia

WE SEE ROWS of telegraph posts every day, and they are so much a part of the landscape of cities and towns that they are scarcely noticed. It takes a beautiful picture like *Road with telegraph poles*, painted by Clarice Beckett, to bring them into focus. When she completed the painting in 1930, such poles had not yet been 100 years in existence. They were a reminder of one of the most important events of 19th century Australia, the coming of the Overland Telegraph.

The first settlers in Australia were 10,000 miles from 'home' and

BECKETT LOVED painting outdoors; she loved the hazy light of early morning and sunset; she loved misty, foggy days. Her subjects were everyday, common scenes: roads, the beach, the sea, the cliffs at Beaumaris.

Nothing could be more ordinary and commonplace than a road, bordered by telegraph poles, winding out of view. *Road with telegraph poles* makes us look, maybe for the first time, at a scene we see every day but to which we barely pay attention. Beckett gives a soft colour and shape to the man-made objects so that they blend with the mellow greens of the grass and trees. The scene is tranquil and yet the telegraph poles and the road are symbols of fast communication, vital to Australia's economic and social development.

Clarice Beckett was born in Victoria. She studied art in Melbourne at the National Gallery School from 1914 to 1916. From 1918 she lived with her parents in Beaumaris, a Melbourne suburb situated on Port Phillip Bay. Beckett was primarily a landscape painter and is recognised as an important modernist artist.

desperate for contact from the outside world. People yearned for letters from Britain and old newspapers brought in by visiting ships. News of great events, like the battle of Waterloo, took months to arrive.

A colonial governor's request for a decision by the British Government would take three months to get to England, with another three months for an answer. Today it would go both ways in seconds, through email and the Internet.

The first break in the isolation was brought by the telegraph. This invention enabled messages in the alphabetical Morse Code (long and short beeps called dots and dashes) to be tapped out and sent along the electric wires. The first messages in Australia were sent between Melbourne and its port of Williamstown in 1854. All the cities, except Perth, were joined up by wires by 1869, with an under-sea cable to Tasmania.

The next step was to join up to the world. England had taken the telegraph line as far as Java (Indonesia). The all-important link for Australia depended on getting an Overland Telegraph line from Adelaide to Darwin, from where under-sea cables would link to Java.

Charles Todd led the army of men that built the telegraph line over 3,200 kilometres of the harshest land. They faced great heat and raging storms, floods that washed away their poles, and termites, which ate all but the hardest wood.

The job of setting 36,000 poles and securing the wire was completed in August 1872, and the under-sea cable link followed. At last Australia could get its news in hours, not months.

DID YOU KNOW?

The central Australian city of Alice Springs is named after the the wife of the leader of the Overland Telegraph project Sir Charles Todd. The 'springs' are situated on land near the meeting of two rivers which flow through the area, and this was the chosen site of one of the telegraph's repeater stations. The rivers were later named the Charles River and the Todd River.

WANT TO KNOW MORE

www.connectingthecontinent.com/ctcwebsite/ctkids/webquest.asp

15. 1901 – The nation is born

AUSTRALIA HAD A huge celebration party when the separate colonies joined together as the Federated nation of Australia on 1 January 1901.

A procession, led by 30 mounted shearers and with soldiers from many countries, marched past banners and flags in Sydney to the site of the proclamation, a white pavilion in Centennial Park.

Before a great crowd, Queen Victoria's proclamation of the nation was read by the Governor-General, Lord Hopetoun, and an interim Government was sworn in. Within a month the Queen was dead after a

Tom Roberts (1856–1931)
Opening of the first Parliament of the Australian Commonwealth, 9th May 1901, 1903
Photogravure
52.9 x 90 cm
National Gallery of Australia

DID YOU KNOW?

The Australian Flag came into being after the federation of the Australian States into the Commonwealth of Australia on 1 January, 1901. The *Commonwealth Blue Ensign* was selected as a result of a public competition in which over 30 000 designs were submitted. It consists of the Union Jack of England, the constellation of the Southern Cross and the Commonwealth star, which has seven points representing the six States and the combined territories.

reign of sixty years, and the nation was in mourning at the opening of the first Federal Parliament in Melbourne on 9 May. The grandeur of the occasion shines in Tom Roberts's monumental painting.

Melbourne's great Exhibition building was decked out for the ceremony and outlined with 20,000 electric lights as the Duke of York (later King George V) declared the Parliament open. Roberts worked from photographs and a preliminary sketch before completing the vast work.

The move towards Federation had begun to gather strength from the time of a meeting of the Australian Natives Association in 1871. The Premier of New South Wales, Sir Henry Parkes, led the way, particularly in a speech he made when the colonies were first linked up by rail. He said then: 'The silver threads of kinship flow through all the iron rails.' He became known as the Father of Federation, but died before the great day.

A GROUP of Melbourne businessmen commissioned Tom Roberts to paint the opening of the first Federal Parliament. His commission required that his painting contain at least 250 likenesses, enabling each one of those individuals to be recognised. This etching was made after he had finished the painting.

Roberts attended the opening ceremony, took photographs, and sketched the scene. Most people at the ceremony were dressed in black as a sign of respect for Queen Victoria who had died in January 1901. National flags and some uniforms of dignitaries and military officers provide the only touch of colour. A shaft of light penetrates the majestic scene, illuminating the Duke of Cornwall and York who is reading the Proclamation from the King.

Tom Roberts called his painting 'The Big Picture'. His friends were concerned about the amount of time he was spending on it and in fact it took him almost three years to complete the painting. Over 5 metres wide, the painting hangs in Parliament House in Canberra. In 1903 the Australian Art Association commissioned printers Goupil and Cie to reproduce the painting in an edition of 500.

WHY DON'T YOU?

Design your own Australian flag.

16. War on our doorstep

IN 1942 A division of young soldiers were rushed to New Guinea to stop a Japanese advance, close to Australian shores. George Silk's photograph *Blinded Soldier, New Guinea* shows a New Guinea volunteer helping a soldier out of the battle area. Japanese soldiers in the north of Papua-New Guinea followed the rough Kokoda Trail to get within 30 kilometres of the capital, Port Moresby. The soldiers of the Australian 17th Division struggled through the jungle and over the mountains, fighting all the way and pushing the Japanese back.

Kokoda was one of many examples of Australians at war. We remember the sacrifices of our servicemen on Anzac Day, 25 April. On that day in 1915 the Australian and New Zealand Army Corps (ANZAC) landed on the Gallipoli Peninsula, Turkey, as part of a British-led force in World War 1.

They fought against German and Turkish forces in an attempt to capture the Peninsula and eventually the Turkish capital of Constantinople (Istanbul). It was an honourable battle against a fierce defender in which thousands of brave men died. The Australians and other Allied forces were forced to retreat by sea. Australians had supported Great Britain in previous wars, such as the Boer War and the Maori Wars, but World War 1 saw our greatest sacrifices. It ended on the battlefields of Belgium and France. By the end of the war Australia was mourning the loss of over 60,000 dead.

During World War 2 the fear that Australia itself would be invaded became a reality. The Japanese landed a powerful blow on 19 February 1942, when 200 planes bombed the far northern city of Darwin.

In New Guinea and on other Pacific islands, American and Australians slowly defeated or isolated the Japanese, and helped to force their final surrender in 1945.

Australian servicemen fought in many countries during World War 2—in the Middle East, in Europe, Asia and the Pacific. Throughout the war 33,286 Australians were killed. More than 180,000 were wounded and 23,000 taken prisoner. Since then we have sent men and women off to war in Korea, Vietnam, Afghanistan and Iraq, and on many peace keeping missions.

George Silk (1916–2004)
Blinded soldier, New Guinea, (Private George Whittington being led to an aid station by Raphael Oimbari), 1942
Photograph
74 x 74 cm
National Gallery of Australia

THIS PHOTOGRAPH shows the bond between Australian soldiers and the Papuans, the so-called 'Fuzzy Wuzzy Angels'.

At the outbreak of World War 2 George Silk took a portfolio of photographs to the office of the Prime Minister in Canberra, and was hired as a war photographer.

Sidney Nolan (1917–1992)
Head of soldier, 1942
Enamel on cardboard
75.8 x 63.3 cm
National Gallery of Australia

SIDNEY NOLAN painted *Head of Soldier* in 1942 when he was serving in the army. At that time he was working on a series of pictures in which he used naive and primitive art techniques to arouse the emotions. *Head of soldier* captures the innocence of a soldier conscripted to fight for his country, the ignorance of the average man about the cause for which he is fighting, and the fear of death. The soldier's mad, rolling eyes and unsteady mouth illustrate the psychological damage war can cause. Although the soldier wears an Australian uniform he is also a universal figure who provokes a condemnation of the cruelty and futility of war.

After the war Nolan toured so-called 'Kelly' country in north-eastern Victoria, travelled to Fraser Island in Queensland, and ventured into Central Australia. His travels inspired series of paintings. By 1950 the famous English critic, Sir Kenneth Clark, described Nolan as 'Australia's only painter'.

17. The land of snow and ice

Jan Senbergs (1939–)
Antarctic night, 1989
Synthetic polymer paint and collage on canvas
202 x 292 cm
National Gallery of Australia

THE ARCTIC AND Antarctic regions still call to adventurers, like those who spend long months in expedition huts such as the one shown in the painting *Antarctic night* by Jan Senbergs.

The big news in 1911 was a race to the South Pole between a Norwegian expedition under Roald Amundsen and a British group under Captain

Robert Scott. Amundsen got there first, on 14 December. He had used Husky dogs to pull his sleds. Scott used mechanical sleds, which kept breaking down, but finally got there. He and his four companions were so weak that, tragically, they died on the way back.

Sir Douglas Mawson, who led an Australasian Expedition in 1912, came back a hero after an amazing survival story. Mawson was journeying with two men, Alexander Ninnis and Xavier Mertz, when Ninnis fell to his death in a crevasse. His dogs and sleds went with him.

Without supplies Mertz slowly grew sick and died. Mawson, also sick from eating dog livers, battled over great plains of ice ridges, against howling winds and in temperatures of -30° Celsius and below.

At one point his illness caused the soles of his feet to fall off, so he bound them back on with bandages. At another point he fell down a crevasse, but his sled stuck to the edge, and he hauled himself back up with desperate strength.

After crossing 150 kilometres alone, Mawson eventually reached an area where food was stored, close to the base camp. He and his base party then had to spend another winter on the ice before they were picked up by ship in December 1913, two years after their landing.

In another saga, English explorer Ernest Shackleton's ship *Endurance* was crushed by sea ice on 21 November 1915. While Shackleton and five others went for help in the largest boat, 22 men sheltered under upturned ship's boats on Elephant Island, living on seal and seaweed stew. Shackleton brought a trawler back to get them, 105 days after they had set up their camp.

Antarctica is a much safer place today, with radio and telephone contact, ice-breaking ships, planes and helicopters. There are 40 bases there, with five run by Australia.

THE 'WINTERERS' of the Australian Antarctic Division live in Antarctica over the winter. The viewer looks into the interior of a hut where they spend many long and dark nights in extreme isolation. The men have left, but the room still appears incredibly small and claustrophobic. The walls are covered with a tapestry of 'pin-up' images dating from the 1950s, described by Jan Senbergs as 'Antarctic Pop Art'. The warm, inviting colours of the room contrast with the bleakness of the surrounding landscape. Like a capsule in outer space, this human container offers safety in a hostile environment. Outside the hut, which is surrounded by metal objects and junk, stands a man braving the wind and the snow.

Jan Senbergs travelled to Antarctica in 1987 to discover "we are again squatting on the edge of yet another continent and bringing our cultural baggage with us".

Jan Senbergs was born in Latvia, arriving in Australia in 1950. At 15 he left school and became an apprentice screen printer. The renowned artist, Leonard French, taught Senbergs silk screen printing and encouraged his artistic pursuits

Fred W. Elliott (1928–)
Wind scour, Casey Range, 1997
Lithograph
20.3 x 12.3 cm
National Gallery of Australia

WIND SCOUR, Casey Range shows the incredible power of the wind. The prevailing winds have scoured out a plateau next to the rock, leaving a stratified ice cliff. Two people, dwarfed by Antarctica's vast, infinite space, stand near the edge of the cliff. Far in the distance appears the David Range.

Fred W. Elliott was a member of Australian Antarctic expeditions in 1953, 1955 and 1958. He was weather observer and official photographer. In 1953, when stationed on Heard Island, he began to draw. His photographs captured the beautiful landscape and the amazing effects of weathering. On his return home from his last expedition, Elliott became an art teacher. He always intended to 'do something' with his photographs but only upon retirement in 1990 did he complete a series of lithographs based on them. The lithographs were published in 1997 under the title *Antarctica in Black and White*.

18. The great depression

Russell Drysdale (1912–1981)
The rabbiter and his family, 1938
Oil on canvas,
61.5 x 76.7 cm
National Gallery of Australia

IN 1929 THE financial world crashed. Many big businesses were ruined, people were reduced to poverty, and millions lost their jobs in a terrible time known as The Great Depression. The crash started on the Wall Street stock exchange in New York, USA, and caused a succession of crashes in other countries, including Australia. As some economists put

DURING THE Depression many country people survived by eating rabbits (referred to jocularly as 'underground mutton') and by selling their skins. Drysdale's picture captures those years and yet the family looks defiant and even comfortable in their environment. The mother holds a chubby, healthy baby. Vegetables are growing and there is water in the tank. The family will survive.

Drysdale loved the Australian country and its people. He described the vast, ancient land as strange and peculiar. It excited him. *The rabbiter and his family* is an important early work inspired stylistically by artists such as Picasso and Modigliani.

Russell Drysdale was born in England. Relatives lived in Australia (Drysdale's grandfather had emigrated in 1875) and the family settled permanently in Melbourne in 1923. After finishing school Drysdale worked as a jackeroo and station manager. This would have been his life if a detached retina had not taken him to hospital where, to keep boredom at bay, he drew. His doctor showed his work to the noted artist Daryl Lindsay and consequently Drysdale began to study art, first in Melbourne, then in London and Paris.

it: 'Wall Street sneezed and Australia caught a cold.' The sombre mood of the Great Depression is caught in Russell Drysdale's painting *The rabbiter and his family*.

With the slow-down of money and markets, many businesses closed in Australia. Australia's unemployment rate was the second highest in the world. Families had to subsist on what money they had saved, and any part-time work they could get. Those who could not pay the rent were thrown out of their houses, and shanty-towns were built on the outskirts of the cities, at places like Homebush in Sydney, the Dudley Flats in Melbourne and by the Torrens River in Adelaide. People lived in humpies made of wooden boxes and tin.

Men roamed the land looking for work, anything from odd jobs to farm labouring. They tramped the roads together and lived in camps, surviving on what food they could get. Luckily, the rabbit plague enabled the cooking of many a rabbit stew over the campfires.

The Government introduced sustenance pay—known as 'the susso'—to help people survive. Special projects like roadworks and landscaping helped to provide jobs. The Melbourne retailer Sidney Myer was among the wealthy people who helped the poor. He paid for the creation of the Yarra Boulevard, which runs through parkland by the river.

Slowly the world worked its way out of the financial crisis and Australians got back to work. The Great Depression was over by 1933, but the memory of it stayed with those who had lived through it, creating a generation of thrifty people who understood the importance of owning a home, and thought that debt was a sin.

WHY DON'T YOU?

Talk to an old person – a neighbour or relative perhaps – who lived through the Great Depression, and write about what they tell you.

19. The opera house: a modern wonder

THE SYDNEY OPERA House is one of the world's most famous buildings. It is as well known as the Eiffel Tower in Paris, the Statue of Liberty in New York or the Colosseum in Rome. The Opera House became such a popular object of interest that it appeared in all sorts of paintings and pictures, including Eric Thake's kitchen-sink version *An Opera House in every home.*

The Opera House was finished in 1973, 16 years after the project was

Eric Thake (1904–1982)
An Opera House in every home, 1972
Linocut
13.8 x 21.3 cm
National Gallery of Australia

announced. The New South Wales Government had a competition for the design of an Opera House. The judges had to choose a winner from 232 designs, and selected the one by Danish architect Joern Utzon.

Utzon's series of sail-like roofs looked brilliant, but the details still had to be worked out. Disagreements with the Government caused Utzon to resign in 1966, and the project was completed without him. The cost blew out from the original estimate of $3.5 million to $50 million. The Opera House is a theatrical showplace, but its true glory is its site at the heart of Sydney Harbour. It stands above the sparkling waters next to the busy ferry terminal at Circular Quay and opposite the Sydney Harbour Bridge, which was a world wonder itself when it was completed in 1932.

IN 1941 Eric Thake printed Christmas cards from lino blocks for his friends. A tradition began which Thake maintained for the next thirty odd years. His cards reveal a delightful, wry sense of humour. *An Opera House in every home* is perhaps the best known. The Sydney Opera House, a masterpiece of massive, curving shapes, is reduced to a stack of plates and a cup on a drying rack. Port Jackson is a ripple of washing-up water.

Eric Thake was born and lived in Melbourne. He studied art under George Bell who was an important influence on many artists (including Russell Drysdale). Thake left traditional landscape painting to become a modernist and a surrealist artist. He worked on small-scale works – paintings, prints, drawings, watercolours and photographs. Except for a period during World War 2 when he served as an official war artist, he earned his living as a graphic designer. Thake's works have been described as 'one of the best-kept secrets in Australian art'.

DID YOU KNOW?

Joern Utzon's historic resignation from the Opera House project caused a furore of protest. There were rallies and marches to Sydney Town Hall and other architects resigned their profession and became teachers, chefs, film makers and artists. The Victorian Chapter of the Royal Australian Institute of Architects (but not NSW) black banned the replacement of Utzon by an Australian architect.

20. The cities get complicated

Jan Senbergs (1939–)
Port Liardet Limner, 1992
Etching
119.4 x 89.2 cm
National Gallery of Australia

THE SCENE IN *Port Liardet* by Jan Senbergs, with the West Gate Bridge curving away from the chaos of Melbourne, is an expression of the dehumanising effect of big cities.

In the 1950s, choking traffic in the cities brought an urgent need for bigger, wider roads. The Cahill Expressway in Sydney, with its four lanes each way, was Australia's first big response. It swooped over the hill at North Sydney and rose up to the Sydney Harbour Bridge. On the other side it straddled the busy waterfront, and then cut through the Kings Domain to the eastern suburbs or, by an off-ramp, into the city.

In Melbourne in 1965 another scenic area, the Yarra River valley, was chosen to carry the increasing traffic in and out to the south-eastern suburbs. As in Sydney, houses, factories and parklands were taken over for the creation of the Monash Freeway.

Today the road-building projects are even bigger. Sydney was given a tunnel to help get the traffic across the harbour, and a road overhaul for the Olympic Games in 2000 allowed traffic to flow from the airport right to the games site at Homebush, and for easier movement all around the city.

In Melbourne the City Link tunnel and connecting freeways and bridges can carry a motorist 60 kilometres, from Dandenong in the south-east to Tullamarine airport in the north-west.

There are now freeways in all of Australia's cities, even the smallest capital, Hobart, Tasmania. All this is good for drivers in off-peak times, but on working days the freeways are clogged by cars, and an accident can stop the whole system for long, frustrating periods. The wider roads and blocked-off suburban areas also make the inner cities much less friendly places for cyclists and walkers.

WILBRAHAM LIARDET was the first European to settle by the water in an area now known as Port Melbourne. Liardet built a hut, obtained a whale-boat, and carrried mail ashore from ships. Senbergs depicts the 'Port Liardet' of the present: a jungle of metal and robot-like people. In the background appears the beautiful curve of the West Gate Bridge.

Senbergs lived and worked for a time in Port Melbourne where he experienced the dark, industrial side of city life. His sombre paintings and prints record the industrialisation of cities and ports and the overpowering presence of machines.

WHY DON'T YOU?

Draw a map of the roads and freeways near your home.

21. Where the money comes from

David Moore (1927–2003)
Newcastle steelworks, 1963
Photograph
36 x 49.5 cm
National Gallery of Australia

WOOL AND GOLD got the Australian economy off to a great start. There were other minerals, too—silver, lead, zinc and copper—as well as oil and gas reserves and great mountains of iron ore. Coal and the energy of fast-flowing rivers in the east have provided electrical power. The focus now is on new and clean power sources and a clean environment, but David Moore's *Newcastle*

NEWCASTLE STEELWORKS shows the size and strength of BHP's steel-making operations in Newcastle in the 1960s. Two young and fit cyclists are coming over the hill, framed by a lattice-work of power lines, concrete, steel, and smoke. In 1963, most viewers would not have been horrified by this scene of apparent environmental carelessness. The steel works closed down in 1991 after 84 years in operation.

David Moore's love of photography began when he was eleven years old and his father gave him a box camera. At the end of World War 2, Moore began working in Sydney for the famous Australian photographer, Max Dupain. His passion was documentary photography and in 1951 he went overseas to work as a photojournalist. In the 1970s Moore no longer wished to photograph the 'decisive moments' sought by magazine publishers but to capture what he called 'the soft spread of time'.

steelworks was taken in a time when climate change and clean energy were unconsidered ideas.

In the 19th century, New South Wales became an importing colony dedicated to free trade, while Victoria wanted to be self-sufficient and charged duty on imported goods. There were customs agents in the ports and along the Murray River to prevent people smuggling goods from New South Wales into Victoria.

Victoria had many factories, making clothes and shoes, tools, machinery and all manner of goods. For a long time New South Wales lagged behind economically.

With a worldwide move to free trade in the late 20th century, Victoria's factories slowly closed down. For a time it was known as 'the Rust Belt State', but it remained the commercial centre for many big companies.

Modern Australia now has a diverse economy, still with minerals and a productive rural sector at its heart, but with many industries built around smart ideas and technical products. Western Australia and Queensland have risen to the fore as the resource states, while Victoria and New South Wales are strong business and industry states. The national economic resources are divided between oil and gas, minerals, electricity, agriculture, crop production, sheep and cattle, other livestock, forestry, fisheries, industry and commerce, tourism, retailing, finance and service industries.

WANT TO KNOW MORE?

www.dfat.gov.au/aib/competitive_economy.html

DID YOU KNOW?

Australia's small business sector is vital to the economy. There are about 1.2 million small businesses in Australia employing around 3.3 million people. During the past decade, small businesses have created an estimated 660 000 new jobs. They are also important contributors to exports—some 42 per cent of all goods exporters are small businesses.

WHY DON'T YOU?

Write about a business that you would like to run.

22. Life in the ever-growing suburbs

Howard Arkley (1951–1999)
House and garden, western suburbs, Melbourne, 1988
Synthetic polymer paint on canvas
174.7 x 400 cm
National Gallery of Australia

THE 'GREAT AUSTRALIAN dream' is humble enough. It is the idea of a family owning their own home in the suburbs.

Today the suburbs are spreading further and further out and the dream has changed a little. The older working people's cottages of the inner suburbs are the most sought-after homes for people wanting an

MOST AUSTRALIANS live in the suburbs, not in the country. Suburbia fascinated Howard Arkley. He loved it and respected it.

House and garden, western suburbs depicts the suburban dream and reveals the bizarre obsession with a neat and perfect house and garden. The colours are bright and strong; the sky is blue and cloudless; the lawn is flawless; the road and the pathways curve harmoniously; the roof tiles sit in perfect alignment; the multicoloured, striped garage door hides the most functional of structures; and the trees and shrubs grow healthily and tidily in appropriate spots. The ordinary has become extraordinary.

Howard Arkley was born in Melbourne, into the suburban world that would become the major subject of his paintings. At the age of 15 he saw an exhibition of Sidney Nolan's works. He decided he would become an artist. Arkley painted with great care and precision, using all the tools of an artist but acquiring an extraordinary skill with the airbrush. His 'Home Show' at the 1999 Venice Biennale was the pinnacle of his career. Tragically, he died shortly afterwards.

inner-city lifestyle, surrounded by bustling street life.

These homes are often side-by-side with blocks of public housing units, where new immigrants, unemployed and otherwise disadvantaged people live, at least until they can save enough to build their own dream.

Working families have largely gone from the inner city, and often live in outer suburbs up to 50 kilometres away. In these days of two-income families both mum and dad have to work to pay the mortgage. Children have become used to day-care centres and after-school programs.

The outward spread of the suburbs began in the 1920s and 1930s with the coming of affordable housing. Returned servicemen with housing loans built on new estates on the fringes of the city, their suburbs mostly clustered around the train lines. After World War 2 the spread became a headlong rush.

Public transport went further and further out. Separate towns like Windsor in Sydney and Dandenong in Melbourne became regional business centres, and were followed up by gigantic shopping centres with huge car parks.

WHY DON'T YOU?

Write about what you like about your suburb or town?

John Brack (1920–1999)
Segment of a suburb, 1961
pen and ink
37 x 64.6 cm
National Gallery of Australia

JOHN BRACK uses repeated rectangular shapes and textured areas to create an image of a flat, featureless suburb stretching to the distant horizon. His hard-edged style emphasises the uniformity of urban life.

Brack, an artist and teacher, commented on life around him with a distinctive, restrained style. He had great success with his *Collins Street, 5pm.*, which showed lines of grim-faced workers filing home from the office, and its companion piece, *Six o'clock closing*.

As a young man Brack worked in an office and studied art at evening classes, turning to full time study after war service. He was appointed painting master at Melbourne Grammar School and later became the head of the Art School at the National Gallery of Victoria.

In the new suburbs, churches and schools, parks and gardens, sports teams and social groups became part of the social 'glue' that keeps communities together. Places like shops, hotels and cinemas followed the people. Gardens grew and trees filled the skyline.

Is everyone happy? Well, that is an impossibility, but most people seem to become very fond of the places where they live.

23. Sports mad down under

Ethel Spowers (1890–1947)
Football, 1936
Linocut
22.6 x 27.6 cm
National Gallery of Australia

CRICKET WAS INVENTED in England, and it infuriated the English when those colonial Australians began to beat them at their own game. The first English cricket teams played 11 men against Australian teams of 20. Soon it was 11 against 11, and in December

THE PLAYERS in *Football* are frozen in mid action. The lines and the curves of the bodies and arms express the dynamism, the strength, and the grace of the players and lead the eye to the focal point of the picture – the ball.

Ethel Spowers was born into a wealthy family in Melbourne. She spent a brief time in an art school in Paris before undertaking a course in drawing and painting at Melbourne's National Gallery School. She became an illustrator of fairy tales. Her work underwent a radical change when she studied under Claude Flight at the Grosvenor School of Modern Art in London. Flight enthusiastically promoted mass-produced linocuts, a 'democratic' and affordable medium using ordinary household linoleum. Flight believed that a work of art should cost little more than a cinema ticket. When Spowers returned to Melbourne she became a founding member of the Contemporary Art Group.

1877 an Australian team beat England in Melbourne. The match had been promoted as a 'Test' between the nations.

The continuing Test series against England became known as The Ashes Series. The name arose from a mock obituary in the English *Sporting Times* after a series loss in 1882, which stated that: '*English Cricket died at The Oval on 29th August. The body will be cremated and the Ashes taken to Australia.*'

The greatest cricketer yet to play was Australia's Sir Donald Bradman. He had the highest batting average of any Test cricketer at 99.8 (he was bowled for a duck in his last innings and so was denied an average of 100 or more.) Bradman began his Test career in 1930 and retired as Australian captain after the 1948 Ashes series in England.

The most watched game in Australia, Australian Rules Football, is a completely home-grown Australia sport. Its rules were first codified in the 1850s by a group of sportsmen, including William John Wills. Some people believe the game was adapted from a kicking game played by local Aboriginal people with a stuffed possum skin for a ball. It also has many similarities to Gaelic Football.

Australian Rules Football is hugely popular in Victoria, Tasmania, South Australia, Western Australia and the Northern Territory. New South Wales and Queensland are devoted to two forms of rugby, League and Union, although both now have AFL teams as well. On the international scene, the Australian Socceroos are enjoying increasing success. Their placement in the top 16 of the 2006 world cup thrilled all sports-loving Australians.

DID YOU KNOW?

Australia's top sports (ranked by percentage of interest) are: Tennis 62, Swimming 61, Australian Rules 57, Soccer 49, Rugby League 44, Rugby Union 42, Motor car racing 34, Golf 30, Athletics 29

WHY DON'T YOU?

Write about playing your favourite sport.

24. In the sun and on the beach

Gert Sellheim (1901–1970)
Australia surf club, c.1936
Lithograph
98.6 x 60.9 cm
National Gallery of Australia

AUSTRALIA SURF CLUB was commissioned by the Australian National Travel Association. It captures the typically Australian images of sun, surf, and sand. The eye catching composition of diagonals and contrasting colours and textures reinforce the text while illustrating the main activity of the surf club—the reel-and-line rescue procedure.

Gert Sellheim's parents were German but he was born in Estonia (at that time part of the Russian Empire). He fought with the White Army (the anti-Bolshevik forces) during the Russian Civil War. He became an architect and migrated to Western Australia in 1926. For a few years he worked as a farm labourer until his qualifications were recognised.

In 1931 Sellheim moved to Melbourne where he worked as an architect and designer. His interior decoration of the Victorian Government Tourist Bureau's building won him the Sulman prize in 1939. During World War 2, he spent some months in an internment camp because of his German citizenship.

Sellheim became an influential graphic designer. He incorporated Aboriginal imagery into his posters, interior decoration and book designs. He created the flying kangaroo logo for QANTAS airlines.

AUSTRALIANS LOVE THE beach and the sea, and the expression 'Life's A Beach' has become part of the language. Gert Sellheim's lithograph, *Australian surf club*, captures all the golden joy of sun and sea.

Swimmers sometimes get into trouble in the surf, but the Surf Life Savers are there to help them. Since the voluntary organisation was started in 1907 at Bondi it has made 512,000 rescues around the Australian coastline. Bondi lifesavers invented the life-saving reel, and the biggest rescue was at Bondi Beach on Black Sunday, 6 February 1938. Around 200 swimmers were rescued after they were sucked out by a vicious undertow. Around 50 were unconscious and five could not be revived.

Our population is drawn to the coastal fringes of the big continent and a dip in the surf. Only the foolish or ignorant swim outside the flags placed by the lifesavers. On summer weekends the city beaches are lively, and beach resorts are crowded with campers and the lucky owners of holiday homes, some of which are million-dollar mansions.

At the end of the 19th century, public bathing was considered rude. Women used to enter the water in their neck-to-knee costumes shielded by 'bathing machines', cages on wheels that were rolled into the water. At Manly, Sydney, in 1902, William Gocher took a dip to test the local law that forbade swimming in the daytime. He was duly arrested, but the court case was such a farce that the embarrassed Manly Council had to make changes.

Seaside holidays were believed to be beneficial to the health. With the coming of more leisure time in the late 19th and early 20th centuries, people liked to travel to the grand hotels built at the seaside. They would promenade up and down the seafront and, as rules and public attitudes changed, some would be daring enough to go swimming.

Today the beaches of Australia are a summer playground not only for swimming and surfing, but also for sunbaking and paddling, beach cricket and volleyball, or just reading a book under a beach umbrella.

DID YOU KNOW

Australia's most famous beach is Bondi Beach seven kilometres from the centre of Sydney. Bondi is believed to be an Aboriginal word meaning the sound of breaking waves. Bondi is known throughout the world and attracts millions of tourists each year, as well as the locals who enjoy the surf and the wide, golden sands.

Max Dupain (1911–1992)
Sunbaker, 1937
Photograph
38.6 x 43.4 cm
National Gallery of Australia

THE BEACH, a favourite place for Australians, provided the scene for Dupain's famous photograph, *Sunbaker*. Dupain, too, considered the photograph one of his best. The close-up, low-angle shot produces a striking, intimate image. The composition not only gives the man's head, arms and shoulders a classical symmetry but also simulates a landscape – a mountain rising out of a plain.

Max Dupain was born and lived in Sydney. He fell in love with photography at the age of 13. In 1928 he joined the Photographic Society of NSW and began working as an apprentice in a photographic studio. During World War 2 he served as an official war photographer. In the early 1930s he opened his own studio and became a successful and celebrated photographer.

Dupain loved Australia and the intensity of the light. His style was modern and innovative; black and white his favourite medium. The breadth of his work was extensive – people, the countryside, cities, fine buildings, and industry.

25. People from all over the world

David Moore (1927–2003)
Migrants arriving in Sydney, 1966
Photograph
24.6 x 26.5 cm
National Gallery of Australia

NINE MILLION IMMIGRANTS have arrived in Australia since the First Fleet landed at Sydney Cove in 1788. They came over many decades, for many reasons and from many places.

In the 1840s there were Scots, thrown off their tenant farms by their landowners, and Germans, who went to South Australia to escape religious intolerance. In the 1840s many thousands of Irish people were forced from their homeland by a potato famine, which caused starvation.

People came from everywhere in the 1850s to join the gold rushes.

Among them were many Chinese, who discovered that they were not welcomed by the largely white population. They were taxed and shunned and finally banned by the White Australia Policy.

This exclusion of all but white people lasted for 70 years, from 1880 to 1950. It was finally abolished after World War 2, when Australia decided it must 'populate or perish'. Even then the immigrants were mainly British and European, people from the Baltic States, Italians and Greeks, Spaniards and Turks.

Things changed in the 1970s with the arrival of 'boat people' from war-torn Vietnam. Immigrants from other Asian countries, and from India, Africa and the Middle East, arrived later, some fleeing war or persecution, others to join their families, and many with skills and ideas to offer the nation.

Our multicultural society encourages people to keep the traditions from their country of origin, while embracing Australian values and Australian citizenship. Our wonderfully varied immigrant intake shows that all people have things of value to offer the country, whether it is their unique food, their music, their ideas or their culture – Australians have embraced the richness that immigrants have brought to our country, despite occasional examples of racism and intolerance. Children play happily together, hardly noticing their differences of origin. They are the ones who will make multicultural Australia an even better place in the future.

Robert Dickerson (1924–)
Migrants in Fitzroy, 1990
Lithograph
56 x 76 cm
National Gallery of Australia

IN HIS recognisably angular style, Robert Dickerson depicts a migrant couple in *Migrants in Fitzroy*. There is a sense from the picture that they are comfortable and successful in their new country, but at the same time pine after their country of birth.

Dickerson is a keen observer, watching with pleasure ordinary people going about their daily business. From his studio in Melbourne he could watch local Italian women, wearing headscarves, gardening and conversing in a communal garden.

Dickerson, born in Sydney, was self-taught and did not start his full-time art career until he was 50. He became one of Australia's most well known figurative artists. He spent half his career as a painter before embracing printmaking, which he considers a viable alternative to the traditional techniques of painting and drawing.

DAVID MOORE was on assignment for the *National Geographic* magazine when he photographed *Migrants arriving in Sydney*. The group of immigrants have dressed well for their first day in their new homeland. Some are anticipating the pleasure of greeting and embracing relatives. Some seem to be wondering with some apprehension about their future in a foreign land, while others seem simply curious or even unconcerned.

David Moore, one of Australia's most prolific and influential photographers, created many iconic images. He was only 22 when he revealed poverty and despair in *Redfern interior*. The photograph was included in Edward Steichen's famous *Family of Man* exhibition held at the Museum of Modern Art in New York in 1955.

WHY DON'T YOU?

Write an essay about your family's racial background and history.

DID YOU KNOW?

Australia is home to citizens from some 200 countries, making it the most multilingual workforce in the Asia–Pacific region. More than 4 million Australians speak a second language.

26. The land—from jungle to desert

William Robinson (1936–)
Creation landscape – water and land II, 1991
Lithograph
56 x 70 cm
National Gallery of Australia

EXCEPT FOR THE coastal fringes, most of Australia is desert, and the country is known as the driest continent on earth. People travelling in outback Australia can go for many hundreds of miles, seeing nothing but flat, red earth and low, scrubby bushes. Even in the inland, however, there are many startling places, some of them world famous for their beauty. In the Northern Territory alone Uluru, Katatjuta,

WILLIAM ROBINSON'S *Creation landscape* series is inspired by the description in the Bible of the creation of the world. *Creation landscape: water and land II* depicts the third day, when God created the seas and the earth. A beam of light strikes the water which fosters a dense forest of trees and plants.

Robinson expresses very personal feelings and experiences through his art. His landscapes reveal his relationship with nature and his belief in a caring guardianship which he calls 'providence'.

William Robinson was born in Brisbane. He is an accomplished pianist and an eminent landscape artist. He studied art and became a teacher of art, retiring in 1989 to concentrate on his painting. His works have won several prestigious art awards including the Archibald Prize (in 1987 and 1995), and the Wynne Prize (in 1990 and 1996).

Katherine Gorge and Kakadu have World Heritage status.

Spectacular formations in the central and western deserts have been caused by the weathering of the central rock plateau over millions of years, leaving cliffs and caves, rocks, spires and canyons as far as the west coast.

On the east coast, the mountains of the Great Dividing Range, from Far North Queensland and Tasmania, bring rain and more varied landscapes. There are snowfields and waterfalls, jungles and rainforest in the tropical north, rivers winding through farmland, hills and valleys, lakes and streams.

Eastern Australia has the wettest country, and torrents of water rush to the sea. William Robinson's *Creation landscape – water and land II* is a dramatic vision of the wealth and abundance of the northern coastal country.

On the western slopes of the Divide the country flattens out, but is fed by the rivers of the Murray-Darling Basin, a great area that holds the most productive farmland in Australia. This great network of rivers has been used to irrigate the land for fruit, cotton, rice and many other crops, but the water flow has become critically short in the drought years from 2000 onwards. Already a great wetland area known as the Macquarie Marshes—an abundant wildlife habitat—has virtually dried up through the over-use of the river waters, and many other natural areas are threatened.

As climate change and global warming take hold, Australians must begin treating water as a scarce and valuable natural resource.

List of Illustrations

Wandjuk Marika (1927–1987)
Rirratjingu people, North East Arnhem land
The birth of the Djang'kawu children at Yalangbara.
1982
147.5 x 66 cm
Ochre on eucalyptus bark.
National Gallery of Australia
© Wandjuk Marika. Licensed by VISCOPY, Australia, 2008.

Benjamin Duterrau (1767–1851)
Mr Robinson's first interview with Timmy, 1840
Oil on canvas
113 x 142 cm
National Gallery of Australia

Benjamin Law (1807–1882)
Trucaninny, wife of Woureddy, 1836
Cast plaster, painted
66 x 42.5 x 25.7 cm
National Gallery of Australia

Abraham Solomon (1824–1862)
Second Class—The parting: 'Thus part we rich in sorrow parting poor.' 1854
Oil on canvas
69.4 x 96.6 cm
National Gallery of Australia

John Wolseley (1938–)
Botanist's camp: tropical night, 1997
Lithograph
74 x 93.5 cm
National Gallery of Australia

Mickey of Ulladulla (c1820–1891)
Untitled. Fishing, native fauna.
Pencil, gouache, watercolour
43 x 68 cm
National Gallery of Australia

S. T. Gill (1818–1880)
Cradling, Forest Creek, 1852
Lithograph
15.2 x 20.6 cm
National Gallery of Australia

William Kelly (1943–)
Still life: Eureka flag, 1981
Dot matrix computer-generated print
5.6 x 9.8 cm
National Gallery of Australia
Gift of the artist 1993
© William Kelly

William Strutt (1825–1915)
*Black Thursday, Melbourne, Victoria, c.*1863
Pencil, watercolour and wash on paper.
14.1 x 25 cm
National Gallery of Australia

Fred Williams (1927–1982)
Burnt landscape II, 1968
Watercolour, gouache, clay, charcoal
56.8 x 76.6 cm
National Gallery of Australia
© Fred Williams. Licensed by VISCOPY, Australia, 2008.

Noël Nicolson (1937–)
Flash flood, 1992
Lithograph
38.5 x 28.2 cm
National Gallery of Australia
© Noël Nicolson

Nicholas Chevalier (1828–1902)
Return of Burke and Wills to Coopers Creek,
1873–1876
Engraving
11.9 x 18 cm
National Gallery of Australia

George Lambert (1873–1930)
Weighing the fleece, 1921
Oil on canvas
71.7 x 91.8 cm
National Gallery of Australia

Jeff Carter (1928–)
Pure merinos, Sydney sheep show, 1961
Photograph
24 x 37.3 cm
National Gallery of Australia
Photograph: Jeff Carter

Tom Roberts (1856–1931)
*Allegro con brio, Bourke Street west, c.*1885–86, additions, 1890
Oil on canvas, mounted on composition board
51.2 x 76.7 cm
National Gallery of Australia and the National Library of Australia

Lloyd Rees (1895–1988)
The Summit, Ball's Head, 1978
Etching
25 x 30.4 cm
National Gallery of Australia
© Lloyd Rees. Licensed by VISCOPY, Australia, 2008.

Sidney Nolan (1917–1992)
The trial, 1947
Enamel on composition board
90.4 x 121.2 cm .
National Gallery of Australia
Gift of Sunday Reed 1977

Sam Byrne (1883–1978)
*Rabbit plague round-up into old mine, c.*1962
Oil on composition board
60 x 61.4 cm
National Gallery of Australia

S.T. Gill (1818–1880)
Wool drays, 1865
from The Australian Sketchbook (Melbourne: Hamel & Ferguson, 1865)
Coloured lithograph
17.6. x 25.4 cm
National Gallery of Australia

J.W. Lindt (1845–1926)
*Ferntree Gully, bullock dray, One Tree Hill, c.*1880–94
Photograph
15 x 20 cm
National Gallery of Australia

Clarice Beckett (1887–1935)
*Road with telegraph poles, c.*1932
Oil on cardboard
23.7 x 18.8 cm
National Gallery of Australia
Gift of Mrs Hilda Mangan 1972

Tom Roberts (1856–1931)
Opening of the first Parliament of the Australian Commonwealth, 9th May 1901 – with remarque of Edward VII c.1903
Photogravure
52.9 x 90 cm
National Gallery of Australia
Gift of the second Lord Tennyson 1960

George Silk (1916–)
Blinded soldier, New Guinea (Private George Whittington being led to an aid station by Raphael Oimbari), 1942
Photograph
74 x 74 cm
National Gallery of Australia

Sidney Nolan (1917–1992)
Head of soldier, 1942
Enamel on cardboard
75.8 x 63.3 cm
National Gallery of Australia
© Sidney Nolan Trust / Bridgeman Art Library

Jan Senbergs (1939–)
Antarctic night, 1989
Synthetic polymer paint and collage on canvas
202 x 292 cm
National Gallery of Australia
© Jan Senbergs. Licensed by VISCOPY, Australia, 2008.

Fred W. Elliot (1928–)
Wind scour, Casey Range, 1997
Lithograph
20.3 x 12.3 cm
National Gallery of Australia

Russell Drysdale (1912–1981)
The rabbiter and his family, 1938
Oil on canvas
61.5 x 76.7 cm
National Gallery of Australia
© Estate of Russell Drysdale

Eric Thake (1904–1982)
An Opera House in every home, 1972
Linocut
13.8 x 21.3 cm
National Gallery of Australia
Gift of the artist 1973

Jan Senbergs (1939–)
The Port Liardet limner, 1992
Etching
119.4 x 89.2 cm
National Gallery of Australia, Canberra.
© Jan Senbergs. Licensed by VISCOPY, Australia, 2008.

David Moore (1927–2003)
Newcastle steelworks, 1963
Photograph
36 x 49.5 cm
National Gallery of Australia
Gift of David Moore 1983
© Lisa, Michael, Matthew and Karen Moore

Howard Arkley (1951–1999)
House and garden, Western suburbs, Melbourne
Synthetic polymer paint on canvas
174.7 x 400 cm
National Gallery of Australia
© The Estate of Howard Arkley. Licensed by Kalli Rolfe Contemporary Art.

John Brack (1920–1999)
Segment of a suburb, 1961
Watercolour, pen and ink
37 x 64.6 cm
National Gallery of Australia
© Helen Brack

Ethel Spowers (1890–1947)
Football, 1936
Linocut
22.6 x 27.6 cm
National Gallery of Australia

Gert Sellheim (1901–1970)
*Australia surf club, c.*1936
Lithograph
98.6 x 60.9 cm
National Gallery of Australia

Max Dupain (1911–1992)
Sunbaker, 1937
Photograph
38.6 x 43.4 cm
National Gallery of Australia

David Moore (1927–2003)
Migrants arriving in Sydney, 1966
Photograph
24.6 x 26.5 cm
National Gallery of Australia
© Lisa, Michael, Matthew and Karen Moore

Robert Dickerson (1924–)
Migrants in Fitzroy, 1990
Lithograph
56.5 x 76.2 cm
National Gallery of Australia
Gift of Jennifer Dickinson
© Robert Dickerson

William Robinson (1936–)
Creation landscape – water and land II, 1991
Lithograph
56 x 72 cm
National Gallery of Australia
Gift of the artist 2002